KT-474-634

To Rob.

Just a little light

reading.

Ann & Brian

'Xmas '85.

THE SEA DOG'S GUIDE TO BETTER FEEDING

by
RICHARD GRAHAM
with the culinary expertise of
Rachel Lever
and (hopefully) a foreword by
The Rt Hon Edward Heath, MBE, MP
and illustrations by
DON GRANT

Pedigree Books
London
1985

© Richard Graham 1985
Illustrations © Don Grant 1985

First published in Great Britain
by
Pedigree Books
23 Wandsworth Bridge Road
London SW6 2TA

ISBN 0 948654 02 3

Printed and bound in Great Britain by
Anchor Brendon Ltd, Tiptree, Essex

For
Those in Gastronomic Peril on the Sea

CONTENTS

AUTHOR'S THANKS

I should like to express my gratitude to Guinness, the resident ship's cat aboard **Convoy** and the source of much of my inspiration. Also to Messrs Arthur Guinness Son & Co Ltd, another source of inspiration, and whose AGM at the Park Royal Brewery I once brought to an abrupt halt by an irreverent remark.

To Charles Gotto, proprietor of **Convoy** and all who sail in her, to Thames Water for not having charged me any water rates for the past twelve months. To Mr Kenneth Livingstone, for presumably having instigated the repainting of Wandsworth Bridge in such attractive colours. To the Rt Hon Edward Heath, MBE, MP, for having made sailing such a popular pastime. To the British Cat-Fancier's Association and the girl in 'The Ship' at Wandsworth who served me last night with a packet of pork crackles with which I won the confidence of the house cat.

To my good friend Bill of Chelsea Fisheries who sold me an exceptionally good lobster the day after I finished the book (it was a Tuesday, when fish-shops reopen after the weekend) and with it I bought a bottle of a delicious new 1979 Charles Heidsieck champagne, which has just appeared on the market and is called 'Champagne Charlie', presumably because it is for the likes of me!

My heartfelt thanks to all wholesalers, retailers and private customers who buy one or more copies of this book, as well as thanks again to the Rt Hon Edward Heath, MBE, MP, for not having after all written the fore-word and leaving me to do it in my own inimitable way.

Lastly, because she came on the scene last, my heartfelt thanks to Rosie Potter, who in the nick of time took the photographs which adorn the dust jacket and saved me from 'commercial' photography.

Don Grant and Rachel Lever will be suitably thanked by way of royalty cheques for their invaluable help in the making of the volume.

Cat and Mousse

FOREWORD

As I said on the title page, hopefully there would be a Foreword by the Rt Hon Edward Heath, MBE, MP. This morning I had a very nice letter from him dated June 28th and written on House of Commons stationery.

He says "[he is] honoured that [I] should ask [him] to write a short Foreword, but feels he must decline as [he is] concentrating on [his] own writing at present, for which [he] already has a publisher."

This is a pity because I had suggested that Pedigree Books might follow up 'The Sea Dog's Guide to Better Feeding' with Mr Heath's own memoirs — the book he is currently writing — and I had been looking forward to Don Grant's illustrations of life aboard *Morning Cloud.*

However, I suppose you can't have everything, and Mr Heath thanks "[me] for offering the services of [my] firm."

Actually, if Mr Heath would teach me the ropes of seamanship, I would teach him the ropes of publishing and how you can make a great deal more money by being your own publisher than just the author.

Pity, but on the next pages with the author's thanks, I have duly expressed my gratitude to Mr Heath.

R.G.

INTRODUCTION

When you are an author, people keep on asking you **why** you write books. There is a fairly obvious answer, but if you look at the back jacket flap of this one, you will see it is not applicable in my case. But it's better than working in a bank Monday to Friday, and gives one a marvellous sense of insecurity.

How do you write them? Straight onto the typewriter if you want to know, an Olympia portable I bought second-hand at Metyclean in Victoria Street for £25 fifteen years ago, and have charged against tax ever since, though I have no idea what its written-down value is now. Before that I had a Royal with a Spanish keyboard, which my father gave me when I was an undergraduate: I sent it to be overhauled and some fool anglicised the keyboard, ripping out all the ñs and lovely words like 'mayaculos', after which I couldn't bear to look at it again.

Yes, but **how** do you write? Do you have a regular routine? No. That's why I don't work in a bank. I don't go through from breakfast until I have a glass of sherry before luncheon, then take my dog for a walk round some country lanes and after tea revise what I have written in the morning and tear most of it up and then after dinner read the results out to my wife for her comments. I haven't got a wife, I have various lady friends off whom I bore the pants by reading bits to them at odd times of the day and night, or leaving pages in their homes in the vain hope they will read them while I'm not there. At least **they** can't divorce me for it.

So when **do** you write? Sometimes in the middle of the night or the very early morning, times when I'm not likely to be out enjoying myself.

How long does it take you to write a book like this? Apart from this bit, which I'm doing while I wait for a Marks & Spencer's Ocean Pie to heat in the oven for supper, it took me eight hours, from 8 a.m. to 2 p.m. on Saturday, June 8th, 1985 and from 3 to 5 p.m. on the following

Monday. I had a break on Sunday, because my father was brought up in the western isles of Scotland, where work, including cooking, was frowned upon on the Sabbath.

Of course I'm not allowing for the time I shall have to spend on spelling mistakes and grammatical errors, but otherwise this is accurate. Pleasure with leisure has always been my motto in life.

How did I come to write it? Well, I went into 'The Ship' in Wandsworth on Thursday evening (6th June) to have a drink and ask Charles Gotto, who owns *Convoy*, if he would bring the new edition of my 'Good Dog's Cook Book' down from the printers in Essex when the boat was next up that way (the Blackwater River) and deliver them to me by Young's brewery dray from the mooring at Wandsworth Bridge to my house in the Wandsworth Bridge Road. I am sick to death of heavy lorries thundering about the place carrying my books and other commodities, and so would you be if you lived at the top of the Wandsworth Bridge Road.

He didn't seem to mind a bit, and in the course of conversation mentioned that *Convoy* had an excellent lady cook — as I already knew, having sampled and approved her cuisine — and that They were thinking of bringing out a book of *Convoy* recipes. Did I think it was a good idea? I said I would like to think about it and let him know. Actually I was ravenously jealous. We authors don't like other people writing books we might write ourselves. I went away, and on Saturday afternoon sidled back into 'The Ship' and presented him with two-thirds of my manuscript. *This* was how it should be done, I said, rather like Frank Sinatra singing 'My Way', only not saying the words. Yes, he said, meekly, there were too many ordinary cookery books clogging up the market and people were bored by them. It was music to my ears, as was his next remark of would I like a drink.

Of course I had brought His cook into my work, but got her name wrong. Sometimes it was Charlotte and sometimes it was Caroline, because all the lady cooks I know are called Charlotte or Caroline, just as they used to be called Bertha or Bessie or Mrs Bridges, whom I knew in real life as a lady called Angela Baddeley and who now posthumously sells jams and preserves from the grave. Actually it was Rachel, a name which a ballet dancer once said reminded her of the tearing of calico.

We ironed that bit out, and Rachel collaborated with me in revealing her trade secrets to a wider public (Rachel Lever, you will see it on the title page, she can have a reference from me at any time she needs it). I telephoned the printers and Charles arranged a sailing date from Maldon with the books.

The only disappointment was that we couldn't get the Rt Hon Edward Heath, MBE, MP to write a foreword, which is why the page before this nearly had to be left blank.

The next question is if you can write a book like this in eight hours, why don't you discipline yourself and put in a forty-hour week, like a bank manager, turning out a new book each day? You could have two weeks' unpaid holiday each year and that would still bring you 250 new titles each year. Even if you say you only get £240 a throw in Japan, that would give you an annual income of £60,000 and you could stop grumbling about money.

The answer is that there are dangers inherent in over-producing a novel idea, as Sir Clive Sinclair now knows to his cost, and the book market will not absorb more than so many titles each year by any one author, however well known. I suppose I could write under a series of noms-de-plume, like Denise Cartland, Barbara Robins, Susan Jacqueline, etc., but would people buy my books if they didn't know who I was?

Any more questions?

R.G.
12.vi.85

THE SIX THOUSAND DOLLAR BREAKFAST

At the time of going to press, the cost of a breakfast party on board *Convoy* is £8.50 per head. I once had one that cost $6,000 just for me alone.

Even in those days I was keen on transporting people and goods by sea, and in order to get from Dublin to Paris, I had nosed out the fag-end of a liner's west-to-east trans-atlantic crossing. The ship was *The America*, and it sailed from Cobh to Cherbourg, and was, I believe, the same ship that brought over Laurel and Hardy a year later, to be greeted in the Irish city by carillons of church bells (of both denominations) playing 'their' tune.

I had a four-berth cabin in the tourist-class, just like on *Convoy*, but fortunately unshared with anyone, and on the morning of disembarkation I left my baggage out and went to breakfast in the dining saloon. A very good breakfast it was too, with things like fresh orange juice we hadn't had for years, and a most attentive black steward who pressed the US Lines' hospitality on me. The only thing that surprised me was that there weren't more people in the room — I was the only one.

As I continued to heap my plate in good American style, a smartly uniformed ship's officer came up to my table and asked if I was Mr Gray-ham. I said yes and wished him a good-morning (it was only about 7 a.m.) as I downed another cup of good American coffee.

"Didn't anyone tell you to go on shore?" he snarled. I said emphatically not and that I was still finishing my breakfast.

"Do you realise?" he shouted, "That you've held this ship up in Cherbourg for over half an hour and it's cost the line six thousand dollars in demurrage charges."

I suppose I should have told him to send the bill to my parents but instead I followed him to the deck and the waiting tender below with its cargo of sleepy Americans who had been waiting in the dawn cold for over half an hour. I was not spoken to.

The dollar was then four to the £, and taking into account inflation and the rise of the former and the fall in the the latter, a similar breakfast today would work out at around £50,000-£60,000.

Let Charlotte describe something very special she can do only for £8.50 in present-day money.

Per person   1 pork and herb sausage
2 rashers back bacon
1 slice white bread
2 halves of tomato
3 large mushrooms (preferably picked that morning from the water meadows adjacent to *Convoy*, or failing that flat black caps)
3 slices black pudding
1 egg
2 oz baked beans

In a very heavy frying pan heat a little vegetable oil and in the order listed fry all the ingredients except the egg. Clean the pan and in 1 oz butter fry the egg. Plate up and heat the baked beans in the butter with a little Worcestershire sauce.

P.S. She's said nothing about beverages, toast, etc., but they're included in the price.

R.G.

I have only ever once been a ship's cabin boy. I signed on at a place called Astillero, just up the bay from Santander in Northern Spain. We were carrying a cargo of iron ore for the steelworks in Port Talbot, South Wales.

The ship was a brand-new one, and my duties were to occupy the owner's cabin with private bathroom up on the starboard side, facing the sharp end. It was a very correctly run ship, and not even the officers ate with the captain, only the cabin boy.

The reason wasn't *that*, but simply that the captain was too grand to eat with anyone but the passenger(s) and I was not only the cabin boy but the passenger, paying £7 for the privilege. I had to be the cabin boy as well, because the ship was not licensed to carry paying passengers.

It was a glorious experience, though the anti-climax came when I was arrested by a policeman on Port Talbot Docks as an illegal immigrant. Actually all I was doing was going to the Post Office to collect the train fare back to my home port in Suffolk, having radioed my father to telegraph it to me.

For a long time the policeman, having observed me come off the ship, was convinced I was Danish. I am not, though the ship was, and the food too. Oh the food, after the greasy fried hake of Northern Spain.

If I can get a large cabin on *Convoy*, with its own bathroom, I think I shall sign on again as cabin boy, but in the meantime here is the ship's recipe for smorgasbord or hors d'oeuvres as Rachel prefers to call them.

Rachel's recipe for smorgasbord was a laverbread and Guinness roulade, which frankly is long and complicated, and with typesetting at £7 per page and space running short, I have omitted it and suggest instead a smorgasbord-type selection of tit-bits like samphire (see p. 44), gulls' eggs (in season), authentic Danish smoked sprats, and so on.

R.G.

During the course of a much-maligned classical education, I stumbled my way through Virgil and learned about Charon, who for a small fee ferried people across the Styx. Now *that* was my idea of a good ferry. So was the old Rosslare-Fishguard one, where cars were put on to a flat railway truck, one to each truck, and hauled by a venerable steam engine along the pier to be man-and-crane-handled into the ship's hold. I once travelled it with a newly-acquired ship's figurehead in the back of my car.

But most ferries consisted of a small rowing-boat or a flatbottomed punt drawn on an overhead rope across a river by an old man. We had a private one of these across the Severn when I was at school during the war, and the ferryman — Fred the Ferry — was not called up for the army for years because his description of his occupation misled the bureaucrats into classifying him as a merchant seaman, an occupation exempt from military service.

There was, of course, no drive-on, drive-off service, only a step-on, step-off one, and I was amazed the other day to hear the QE2 described as a 'transatlantic ferry'. Does it too now have this revolting facility and do the diesel fumes of over-sized lorries ascend to the passenger cabins throughout the voyage? If so, better come back by Concorde for the inclusive price offered.

I have never been on the QEs, only the old *Queen Mary*, where there was a lot of caviar going in the ticket price. It appears on *Convoy's* menus too, and I wonder what she does with it . . .

Charges a lot extra, I expect.

I do not, anyway until this book becomes a best-seller, own a yacht of my own, but I was once invited to join a school friend of mine on his brother's in the north of Donegal. It was one of those yachts with sleeping accommodation in the middle, and a tiny bit up the sharp end for me, with a hole in the back in which the helmsman sat.

We set off at first light from the quay, at which Irish schooners still unloaded flour for the bakery beside it, and made our way ten miles up or so through a lough into the open Atlantic, heading for the northernmost tip of Ireland which for some political reason belongs to the South.

My friend said we were going to call in at a village called Culdaff, where **poteen** of a very potent but high quality was made and was available to those in the know. In retrospect I feel slightly shocked, as my friend became later an MP with the third largest majority in the House of Commons, which still prohibits the manufacture and sale of **poteen,** and I expect that his successor in his constituency, the Rev Ian Paisley, would be even more indignant if he knew.

But thinking back on it, I recollect that we had spent the afternoon of the day before in a **shebeen*** a mile over the border from Northern Ireland, owned by someone with the impossible name of Snodgrass — for that part of Ireland — and known locally as Mrs Snodgrass's **shebeen.**

I was just about to turn the helm in the direction of Culdaff when we were joined by a fishing boat, whose skipper passed the time of day with us. He pointed to a pile of evil-looking fish on the deck and asked us if we would like some — they were John Dory fish and quite unsaleable in Ireland where fish is reserved as a penance for Fridays and less of it eaten per capita than in any European country. We shuddered at the sight of the hideous beasts and declined, whereupon the fisherman dumped them into the sea.

22   * An Irish term for an illicit drinking-den.

My friend's brother said we were not going to Culdaff after all. I think he thought the fisherman was a Customs & Excise man in disguise, and we ended up at 8 p.m. in Protestant Portrush, where **poteen** is (or was) unknown, having covered well over 50 nautical miles under sail in the day.

Now that the John Dory is almost in the luxury class, I bitterly regret our action, and Rachel is going to tell you what to do with any John Dory's you may get offered you free off Malin Head.

Skin some fillets of John Dory and cut into 3 inch strips. Marinate for two hours in:

> 1 tablespoon soy sauce
> 2 tablespoons soft brown sugar
> 3 tablespoons vegetable oil
> 1 tablespoon wine vinegar
> 1 tablespoon coconut cream
> 1 teaspoon finely chopped garlic
> 1 teaspoon chopped ginger
> 1 teaspoon chilli sauce

Mix all the above well together.

String the fish onto saté sticks and grill. Serve with plain boiled rice and peanut sauce.

Crab and Winkle Soufflé
(with catnip)

CRAB AND WINKLE SOUFFLÉ

We took the manuscript of this book by sea to the printers, who have a place at Tiptree in Essex, where the jams come from, and I rang the General Manager and asked if we could complete the final stage of the journey on the local train which had lovely coaches with wrought-iron balconies at each end.

"You mean the old crab-and-winkle?" he said, "That's been gone over thirty years."

"But the last time I was in Tiptree, Mr Ketley," I replied, "I came by train."

"I bet you were the only passenger," he retorted.

Well, I was. I was a schoolboy at the time, and the train carried just me and my bicycle. I was absolutely thrilled to have an entire train to myself, and the only way I can get near it now is to charter *Convoy* and go out for a day's sailing with the cook, whom I shall regard as the equivalent of the train's guard.

Here is her recipe for crab-and-winkle soufflé:

Fry six clubbed cloves of garlic very gently in 2 oz unsalted butter for five minutes. Discard garlic and make a roux with 2 oz flour and ¼ pint milk. Simmer for one minute.

Off the heat add ½ lb brown crab meat, the grated rind and juice of two limes — avoids scurvy — 1 tsp tabasco sauce, 2 egg yolks, 2 oz winkles and salt to taste. Fold in 4 stiffly beaten egg whites, pour into a well-buttered soufflé dish and bake for 35 minutes at No 6 (or 400°).

If no winkles are available, try using your loaf.

Unlike myself, Arnold Bennett, the author, at the height of his fame, owned a large yacht, the **Velsa.** After his death it went through some bad times and in the mid-50s was purchased by a man with the appropriate name of Wherry. Mr Wherry had visions of running it as a small but very exclusive cruise ship in the Mediterranean (is it one t and two rs or the other way about?), but he needed publicity.

I was then writing travel articles for the smart glossies, for which you then still had to pay, and I and a photographer friend were invited for a fortnight's free cruise, on condition that we wrote some articles for these, encouraging rich passengers. We would be allowed to keep the proceeds.

We sailed from Monte Carlo, and came up on deck at dawn to find the ship scudding along under sail at a good 9 knots towards Corsica. It was a thrilling experience, even though Mr Wherry had acquired a few rich fare-paying passengers, whom we, being very young, christened the 'grown-ups' and avoided as much as possible. I had a cabin all to myself, as the photographer had brought his wife, who made the unfortunate mistake — for the 1950s — of thinking that mooring bollards were called bollocks.

The food, though of the messed-up foreign variety, was good and the wine flowed freely, at no expense to our free-loading selves, though unfortunately, unlike my photographer friend, I didn't have a wife in every port.

One day, somewhere at sea outside Porto Fino, we saw, I think unusually, a shoal of whales spouting. After the last war, when these harmless creatures weren't protected, they were caught and sold here as a thing called 'snoek', which masqueraded as all kinds of things like, say, beef which tasted rather of fish meal.

Rachel gives now her recipe for turbot masquerading as whale.

She says: "Whale according to Larousse Gastronomique is almost inedible and is now a protected species."

I am not talking particularly about oysters, though Rachel may take these as her cue if it is convenient, but of Venice, where I spent part of my one and only honeymoon (to date). Owing to my penchant for surface travel as a means of self-expression, we went by train and boat, breaking the journey for a night in Dijon, where there was an almighty row from my wife about what I thought was a perfectly good train from Paris. Afterwards we ate a reconciliatory steak and pommes frites in a restaurant round the corner from the hotel, followed by the prix fixe lunch the next day at Les Trois Faisans and another train on to Venice.

Here we had our second maritime experience in the form of a speedboat ride to and from that swish hotel on the Giudecca which the Guinneses (not *Convoy*'s cat's family) then owned, followed a few days later by a Yugoslavian ship down to Dubrovnik. It was a spanking new ship with excellent accommodation but dire food, and wine of the same taste and quality as the red ink I used to get at school before biros were invented. The ship was conducted by a correct but unsmiling commissar whom my wife was convinced was out to get us, and she was even more unhappy when as we came out into the street in Dubrovnik after reporting our presence to the police, a tiny little old man approached us and asked her for an English cigarette.

She accused me of his following us, and once we were installed in our hotel (the Argentina, a further indication of anti-British sentiment), she refused to go out of it again until we left for the ship back a week later. There were no boat-rides down the coast to peer at the shores of Albania and no trips on the narrow-gauge steam trains of Yugoslavia to which I had been looking forward. In the end we came back by plane from a vile airport called Malatesta* — which was 40 miles (or kilometres or something) from the

* Or was it Malpensa — Bad Thoughts?

centre of Milan and translates back into Bad Head or perhaps more colloquially Headache.

It only increased my dislike for air travel, but I must say that the food at the Argentina was exquisite and some of it was most ingeniously cooked in paper bags. I haven't had oysters in paper bags. Yet. Unless you count the time I went out in Sofia (Bulgaria) to buy caviar and got 125 grammes of it for a pound, served in a thin paper bag which I had to cup in my hands all the way back to the hotel to stop it seeping through onto the slushy pavements.

Oysters in Guinness

The first time I went on board *Convoy*, she was moored at her home base, by 'The Ship' on the south side of Wandsworth Bridge.

It was eerie. There was not a living soul aboard. A sack of perfectly good potatoes lay on the floor of the saloon and ranged along a shelf to one side (starboard, I think) there were at least a dozen unopened bottles of decent red wine. The galley showed signs of a meal having been recently prepared.

I looked in all the cabins. There was no sign of human life.

It remains one of the great mysteries of the sea. Various theories have been put forward to explain it. My hypothesis, though unproven, is that the crew were all up in the bar of 'The Ship', drinking.

The best antidote to this is Rachel's Marie Celeste Pie.

Poach ¾ lb skinned fillet of cod and ½ lb smoked fillet of ditto in ½ pint of milk until just cooked.

Fry two large sliced onions in 4 oz butter until soft and add 1 oz flour to make a roux with the milk from the fish. Add ¼ pint white wine, ½ lb whole button mushrooms, juice of a lemon, the chopped-up cooked fish and season to taste.

Put into a suitably sized casserole and top with mashed potato.

Bake at No 6 (or 400°) for 35 minutes and abandon ship before eating, leaving the pie on the table in the saloon.

UNSOLVED MYSTERIES OF THE SEA No. 4
Bain Marie Celeste

When the Rt Hon Edward Heath, MBE, MP made his famous visit to Chairman Mao in 1973, I naturally assumed that he would sail **Morning Cloud** out there and tie up at a buoy somewhere on the Yangtze River, perhaps with the Chairman's ex-opera-singer-wife greeting him with a Chinese rendition of 'I'd Like to Get You on a Slow Boat to China'.

Somehow it didn't work out that way, and before I knew where I was, Mr Heath had descended on Peking in an aeroplane with a whole bunch of Conservatives including Whips, and even his own personal physician, though I had been trying to put him in touch with a good local acupuncturist in case he wasn't well.

I don't know what they did all the time, but I like to imagine Mr Heath in the paddy fields, telling Irish jokes to Chairman Mao in exchange for rice production statistics.

Rachel Lever does wonderful things with rice, including kedgeree, risotto, flied lice and other famous international dishes, and as it is such easy stuff to carry on a boat and keeps well, we are including some of her favourite recipes.

Buttered Rice with Squid and Cashews

In 6 oz butter cook 2 bunches of shredded spring onions, 1 tbs grated root ginger, 1 tbs grated fresh horseradish, 2 crushed cloves garlic, ¼ tsp grated nutmeg and ½ tsp grated cinnamon.

Add ½ lb thinly sliced squid and stir fry the lot as best you can against the motion of the vessel for about a good minute. Then add 3 cups* water and the same amount of

*A deceptive American term which bears no relation to the average English tea cup or Italian coffee cup. Don't get caught like I did when I started using 'The American Woman's Cook Book' but look up some reference book to see what a so-called 'cup' is.

R.G.

long grain rice, stir well and cook over a slow heat until the rice is cooked through (about 30 minutes). Just before serving stir in 6 oz cashew nuts. Season to taste and serve with freshly grated Parmesan cheese.

Budino di Riso con Fichi

In a heavy pan put 2 oz round (or square, if you can get it) rice, ½ pint single cream, ½ pint milk, 1 oz caster sugar, ½ a tsp ground cinnamon.* Stir well and cook slowly on top of the stove, with a lid on the pan, for 45 minutes, then remove lid and continue cooking until the mixture is creamy, stirring about every 15 minutes. Cool and serve with figs that have been soaked and then cooked in real coffee, chilled, and with lightly whipped cream.

*Rachel says ½ a level teaspoon ground cinnamon, but I don't quite know how you get ½ a level teaspoonful of anything. If in doubt ask a policeman (I presume they have river policemen on the Yangtze as well as on the Thames).

R.G.

My great-grandfather, who was a very old man, once went to Cornwall before they opened Brunel's railway bridge across the Tamar in 1859, and then had to walk the rest of the way. He passed a cottage en route, outside which was a sign saying 'Fig Pudding 4d per lb, More Figgier 6d'. He told me this with his own ears, and it just goes to show how close the generations are together if you think about it, and I have translated Rachel's name for the stuff into Italian, as frankly it sounds more exotic than just Cornish Fig Pudding at 4d or 6d per lb.

If anything dreadful happens to me shortly after the publication of this book, would someone make it their urgent business to conduct an investigation along the lines of the ones carried out on Mr Calvi, Pope John Paul I and that unfortunate Bulgarian who got stabbed with an umbrella in Aldwych. But even if it doesn't, and you hear clicks on the line when you telephone me, please advise MI5 *immediately.*

The oddest sea journey I ever read about — it was reported in **The Irish Times** many years ago — was that of the Chinese laundryman from Swansea who was apprehended by H.M. Coastguards as he was making a solo trip eastwards along the coast of South Wales in a small open rowing-boat. You must remember that in those days Chinamen here were mostly into laundry rather than takeaway food, and in fact during the happy period I was attached to the Theatre Royal, York, at the end of the 1950's I had all my things done at a Chinese laundry, appropriately enough in Blossom Street (opposite the Odeon cinema).

It turned out that the laundryman was homesick for his native land, and had borrowed the rowing boat and an ordinary school atlas, intending to make his way back to China by following the coastlines shown in the atlas. The Coastguards wouldn't let him and I suppose nobbled the poor chap over some technicality like not having passed through the appropriate green channel on leaving the country (although it is a not very well known fact that a British subject has a perfect legal right to quit our shores without producing a passport and in normal circumstances cannot be prevented from doing so).

It is rather a pity that he couldn't have gone home on **Morning Cloud** with Mr Heath — I can think of nothing more luxurious than having one's own Chinese laundryman aboard one's yacht, and perhaps Mr Heath could have had his washing done in lieu of passage money.

Anyway, supposing that you behave badly on board **Convoy** and Charles turns you adrift in the open boat, what would the good Rachel give you to eat? I don't think the picnic that Mole and Ratty took on the river in 'The Wind in the Willows' would be quite appropriate, and I leave it to Rachel's sense of justice.

P.S. *The Irish Times* always ran good true stories, and I particularly liked the one about the man who was fined £2 for being drunk in charge of a rowing boat in the Middle of Cork Harbour.

When I was a student in a Spanish monastery outside Santander, I used to take great pleasure in walking along the quays which abut the heart of this rather pleasant city.

One day I was looking up — in admiration — at a British merchant ship when I was approached by two very small Spanish boys who asked if I was from England. Actually I was then from Ireland, but as 'Irlanda', of which no-one in Spain had heard, sounds very much like 'Holanda', it only causes confusion and I said 'Yes' ('Sí').

Did we get plenty to eat in England, they asked. Actually we didn't because although the idea had been that when U-boats ceased sinking British merchantmen, we could have as much as we liked, we didn't because Britain was ruled by people like the late Sir Stafford Cripps who liked austerity for its own sake, and food rationing went on until 1952.

The Spaniards, under Franco, had a similar system called 'abastacimiento' — try pronouncing it — and foreign visitors had to spend hours queuing in awful government offices to get food coupons issued before they could have anything to eat. The average Spaniard's difficulty, however, was that when they got the coupons, they had no money with which to buy the food.

These two little boys were hungry.

"But surely, senor," they protested, "you can have all you want to eat in England."

"We can have as much bread and potatoes as we like," I said — this was before Sir Stafford Cripps clamped down on these two items — "but not much else." I explained this in the Spanish I was supposed to be learning at the time.

"Oh, senor," they said, "if only *we* could have as much bread and potatoes as we liked . . ."

I climbed the gangplank and sought out the ship's cook, explaining the situation.

"What time do you serve lunch?" I asked.

"Noon," he said succinctly.

I arranged with him to serve two good hot duty-free midday dinners to the two small boys, came down the gangplank to tell them to wait there until 12 p.m. and went off having done my good deed for the day.

Now supposing you find yourselves penniless in a foreign port with only some potatoes and stale bread on board. What would you do? I will allow you some Spanish onions with which to work out the problem.

Rachel says:

Boil the potatoes in lightly salted water. Drain. Mash.

Peel and slice the Spanish onions and chop the stale bread into cubes.

Beg, borrow, find or steal just ¼ pint of oil* and very gently fry the cubes of bread until golden. Drain and then fry the onions.

Pile the onions on top of the potatoes, the bread onto the onions and accompany with steaks and Sauce Madere.

*Engine sump oil will do if you have an ambulance standing by and are covered by your BUPA subscription.

R.G.

This is absolutely typical. I had photo-copies of my letters made at the time of writing, but of course page 1 would disappear. I wonder if MI5 have been in and at my files? Anyway, you can see that I **did** send the stuff to Belmullet.

-2.-

Anyes? I addressed them to you at Belmullet as I did not then know for sure that you would be unable to take up my suggestion of taking a holiday there to recuperate after our unsuccessful General Election. However, I did take the precaution of asking the postal authorities in Belmullet to forward the package on to you should you be unable to collect it in person. I never heard what happened, but I imagine that the rumour of your imminent - and indeed eminent — coming must have caused quite a stir of excitement in that remote part of County Mayo where they do not have a great deal to occupy their minds.

Now to the main course. This was un pain d'écrivisses. This was not bread with shrimps, as might be served at, say, Broadstairs*, but a delicately flavoured quenelle made with ▬ freshwater crayfish

In 1974 I was ineffectually looking after three British dance troupes for whose presence I was responsible at the Angers Festival, and the days left plenty of time for exploration of the many superb fish restaurants in which the Loire region abounds.

I was on pretty good terms with the Mayor of Angers, and on his behalf had extended an invitation to our ex-Prime Minister, the Rt Hon Edward Heath, MBE, MP, to bring *Morning Cloud* up the Loire on a semi-civic visit to Angers. I received no reply, probably because he was out sailing at the time with his gallant all-male crew, but I had the kindness to parcel up a little selection of shellfish left over from one of my luncheons and send it to him Post Restante, at a place called Belmullet in Co. Mayo, in the hope that his evident love for Ireland would bring him to that little port and he would go ashore for a half-pint of Guinness and to see what mail awaited him in the Post Office. I even went so far as to have *Morning Cloud* translated into Irish — it is 'Scamail ni Madden'.

Belmullet is an incredibly remote place. The nearest railway station is at Ballina, 40 miles away, and until 1940 the roads were so bad that a steamer called *The Tartar* ran there regularly from Sligo, conveying goods and passengers, after which it was sold to Greek owners and sank like a stone on the way out to Crete. It was a very old ship, even older than *Convoy.*

Well, nothing happened, but knowing what Post Offices in small Irish villages are like, I reckon it must have given Belmullet quite a *frisson* to think that Mr Heath was on his way to pay them a visit, and I have often wondered if when the contents of the packet began to putrify, they sent it on to 10 Downing Street and let the then Mr Wilson forward it on to Broadstairs.

I never heard from Mr Heath, but on the facing page is a facsimile of my covering letter to him, and now here is Rachel's recipe for Sauce Tartare:

To ½ pint mayonnaise add:
4 finely chopped gherkins
12 finely chopped capers
1 level tablespoon finely chopped onion
1 level tablespoon finely chopped parsley
½ level tablespoon finely chopped green olives
12 turns of the pepper-mill

I have never been seasick. It is not so much that I think of it as 'unmanly' — in itself a sexist word which ought to be banned — as un-British, and I can remember my father walking me round the decks of the ship on the roughest Folkestone-Boulogne crossing for two years while we looked askance at the behaviour of the other passengers. *

I once felt 'queasy', but that is a different matter, and was brought on by diesel fumes because my lady companion, on a bumpy run aboard the M.V. *Scillonian* from Newlyn to St Mary's (Penzance could not be got into) insisted on going below to partake of what they passed off as mid-morning coffee, while I wanted to stay on deck and enjoy the fresh air.

But seasickness is more a state of mind than anything else, and is of course to be associated with foreigners. In the days when I knew Madeira, there were few roads and most places outside Funchal had to be approached on foot, by donkey or by sea. One day I discovered that there was a boat that sailed from Funchal, past Vila de Lobos to what turned out to be a disgusting little town at the other end of the island.

I bought my ticket and went on board. The boat lay on a flat calm in the inner harbour and the engines had not yet been turned on. Yet the passengers (I was the only non-Madeiran) were already retching and vomiting, holding their heads over the sides and making piteous noises and I can't help wondering if the same kind of behaviour has ever been observed at one of *Convoy*'s stationary Sunday brunches.

Rachel says:

Pan fry in a good olive and vegetable oil 8 oz fillet or rump steaks.

*I think this must have been the time I fought the dragon in the forest at Le Touquet (see p.29 of my 'God Dog's Cook Book') — R.G.

Keep warm on a plate in the oven.

To the pan add to each steak cooked 3 fluid oz Madeira and 4 green peppercorns. Crush the peppercorns into the pan while it's boiling furiously and reduce the liquid and sediment to a third of the original volume. At this stage add 1 tablespoon of sour cream per steak. Boil again.

This luxury may well be served with the recipe from Hard Times.

More Sauce, Madère?

I imagine I must be the only person ever to have eaten samphire off the marble console table in the Piccadilly entrance of the Ritz Hotel.

There were just four days to go before the typescript of this book was due at the printers and I had promised Rachel some of the stuff* to experiment with. The only place it can be found is on the salt sea marshes of the north Norfolk coast, confined to a patch between Wells-next-the-Sea and Cley, but I have a friend who lives near and quite by chance that evening he was bringing me up a Dublin University MA gown and hood for me to wear at a Cambridge dinner the following night (I have never been able to afford one of my own and had to resort to a hire firm for my graduation ceremony).

We were to meet at the Ritz Bar at 7 p.m. and have a drink with two important Japanese booksellers, and I sent him an urgent message asking him to gather some samphire and bring it with him.

In the morning, by when he had already left north Norfolk, by some chance bordering on the para-normal, I saw some of this rare plant in the fishmongers a hundred yards from my home down the Wandsworth Bridge Road. I bought it, and in case my friend had been unable to find any, put it in a plastic bag which had until recently contained a loaf of Sainsbury's wholewheat bread (unsliced).

I had an hour's sleep and then set off for the Ritz with the samphire and two of my books in Japanese translation. The Ritz Bar was chaotic. I could not find my friend, because the lobby had become a cat-walk, not for the ship's cat Guinness, but for a troupe of elegant young mannequins who were pirouetting about in extremely expensive Zandra Rhodes dresses, watched by Zandra Rhodes herself from a table where she was drinking champagne instead of, as I had imagined, being in the changing room fussing about with pins and needle and cotton.

There was no vacant table I could occupy until my friend

arrived, and I kept getting mixed up with the mannequins. In the lobby were two Japanese businessmen in dark suits carrying heavy briefcases. They might have been my friend's friends, also looking for him, but the thought occurred to me that perhaps they were IRA bombers who had been through the hands of a skilled make-up artist and were hoping to interpolate their wares into the Ritz in this guise.

I was torn between ringing the Terrorist Squad and asking them straight out if they too were looking for my friend. But supposing they said yes and then bundled me into a dark cupboard with my Japanese books and the samphire? It doesn't keep fresh very long.

To avoid colliding again with the models, I walked out of the Arlington Street entrance of the Ritz and in through the Piccadilly one. It was then that I noticed there was a hole in the plastic bag, and that bits of samphire were dropping through it onto the delicate pink carpet below. I put the bag down on the console table and ate the samphire that had oozed out of it onto the marble top, hoping that the bits on the carpet wouldn't get trodden in by the crowd.

My friend arrived and eventually we got a table. The Japanese booksellers were surprised to find my work translated into Japanese. I was careful not to say much because it came as a surprise to me to find that the principal industry in Korea is steel-making rather than basket-weaving and rice, and I did not want to embarrass my friend. After my second glass of champagne, I asked if there was a Japanese equivalent of north Norfolk. They said it would probably be West Japan. This only confused me because that far round Mercator's Projection I have no idea which way is west and whether Japan's answer to north Norfolk would be on the left or right side of the country as you looked at it on the map.

Presently we all came out and took a taxi to a restaurant. I passed round the bag of samphire, thinking it would be an excellent substitute for seaweed. Nobody ate much.

Over dinner, as I know nothing about Japan and

45

whether it is friendly towards its Russian neighbours, I kept a tight rein on my tongue, but eventually loosened up and taught everyone to say "I do not understand Bulgarian" in Bulgarian.

Afterwards we all went to Annabel's, where I nursed the samphire and the books in Japanese, and eventually my friend and I decided not to risk driving our cars home, so we walked back to the Ritz and put the samphire and the books on top of the MA gown in mine. Then we shared a taxi home.

After 2½ hours uneasy sleep I took the first underground train from Fulham Broadway to Green Park (charging 60p against my income tax) and recoverd the car. I had been worried about its getting bombed or blown up by the police during the night, but the MA gown and the Japanese editions and the samphire were still safe, and I drove home and went back to bed until it was time to deliver the precious vegetable to Rachel aboard *Convoy*.

---

*The plant *Crithmum maritimum* (growing on rocks by the sea), the aromatic, saline, fleshy leaves of which are used in pickles. Also called Rock samphire. "Halfe way downe Hangs one that gathers Sampire; dreadfull Trade" — Shakespeare (OED).

The **United States**, flagship of the US Lines, was said to be the fastest passenger ship in the world and broke the Blue Riband in 1952 in 3 days, 10 hours and 40 minutes, its real top speed being a military secret.

How I came to be eating pumpkin pie aboard it in mid-Atlantic in October 1964 was that it was Thanksgiving Day, and my wife was in her cabin being seasick, so that I had to have dinner alone with my infant daughter's nanny whom we had brought along. She wore an emerald-green paper hat, which was one of our perquisites of this celebratory American evening and contrasted badly with the sea-sick pallor of her face. I was not very full of the milk of human kindness, having topped up with something else at the bar beforehand, and thought of sending a ship-to-shore radio-telegram to Norland Nanny HQ in England, reporting her for not wearing her regulation headgear in a public place.

However, I managed to keep the conversation stumbling along and we got to the pumpkin-pie stage of the meal. It was quite tasteless, like nearly all the food on board the **United States,** which was designed for 'plate appeal' rather than the human palate.

Afterwards I was invited to see round the ship's kitchens, an honour which rather appealed to me. They were extraordinary. Dozens of chefs standing around in spotless white hats and aprons, acres and acres of highly polished stainless steel serving tables, spotless floors, not a cockroach in sight, not as much as a milligram of food anywhere. It was rather like a town in Northern Ethiopia today, only cleaner.

Convoy's galley, on the other hand, is open-plan, in fashionable Fulham-farmhouse style, with lots of pine cupboards and oak beams, and is designed to make the passengers, including Guinness, feel really at home, with Rachel's delectable tit-bits decorating the serving counter.

It really ought to be investigated by the Committee for un-American Activities.

The recipe for Pumpkin Pie is:

Boil a large can of condensed milk — needless to say unopened — in water for 3 hours and *see the water doesn't boil away before the time is up.* Cool it before opening, otherwise you may have trouble, and add contents to 1 lb well-drained cooked pumpkin flesh with a pinch of salt, ½ tsp ground cinnamon and ¼ tsp ground mixed spices. Fold in ½ pint stiffly beaten double cream and three stiffly beaten egg whites. Pour into a digestive and ginger biscuit pie case — whatever that is — and dust with grated nutmeg. Afterwards stay in the heads or near the side of the vessel.

Banana Boat Flambé

BANANA FLAMBÉ

In the place I spent my childhood, things moved slowly. Some people had never been on a train, a few others never seen one, having not travelled the eight miles necessary to do so; my own father, though he lived to be 84, never set foot in an aeroplane, and did not wish to do so.

I was only induced to take to the heavens because a firm that ran passenger flying-boats until about 1960, induced me to go on one by offering me a flight at half-price, even though by then I was well over twelve years of age, and when I finally took a 'real' plane, I made sure it was from a grass airfield as I felt that if anything went wrong, it would be softer hitting grass instead of tarmac.

As my neighbour on the flying-boat observed, italicising her words as she spoke, "Somehow it seems much more *natural* coming down and taking off on the water." It is. One minute you are a plane and the next a boat (and vice versa).

It was a lovely experience. How many of my readers have ever flown at 600 feet along the South Coast of England, looking closely into the backyards of Bournemouth and Lymington? How many have ever found themselves the only two literate passengers out of twenty-two, the others being all American citizens unable even to write their names, and spent a journey filling in immigration forms in Portuguese? It pays to be a resident scribe on a flying-boat, I can tell you, and I wish the post was still open.

Eight hours at a steady — and I mean *steady* — 200 m.p.h. is exhilarating in a comfortable armchair, particularly when on taking off for the next lap, a mechanical part is found to be irretrievably broken and it means a free night in a luxury hotel prior to the next one's boarding-house, and a free dinner with a pretty stewardess who tells one of the time when the vehicle hit a submerged rock in Genoa harbour and the passengers were made to stand out on one wing to balance it before it tipped and sank. I particularly liked the old lady who sent her husband back into the hull for her umbrella and gloves because she said she couldn't be seen out of doors without them.

Anyway, I had never seen bananas growing live before, so at the end of the meal I ordered some to be flambé-ed at the table. Charlotte will tell you how to do them, and if you can't get hold of a flying-boat, why not charter *Convoy* instead?

Banana Flambé for one:

Slice banana lengthwise and fry in ½ oz butter on both sides. Remove fruit and keep warm. Add to pan 1 dessert-spoon maple syrup, 1 fl oz Navy rum and ½ fl oz whisky. Swirl pan over high flame, ignite liquid and pour over banana.

Any port in a storm

I said just now that I once had a train all to myself, and now I remember that I have had two ships to myself, one the Danish one and the other the S.S. *Woodlark*, owned by a firm called Moss Hutchinson Lines.

The *Woodlark* had been built in 1924 for the Leith-London run, carying cargo and up to twelve passengers. After the war, when the attempt to revive the Leith-London run was a failure, it was put on the Bristol-Oporto route, still theoretically carrying passengers as well as barrels of port wine. I was the only passenger on a journey scheduled to take 2½ days.

All 900 tons of us sailed out from just behind the Bristol Old Vic and got bumpily past Hartland Point and into the Bay of Biscay, where a strong wind called a Force 9 gale blew up. From 30 nautical miles away a Spanish ship wirelessed to say that it was sinking, and we set off in its direction at a speed of 2½ knots, the captain explaining that any more would break the ship's back. The worst part of it was that in those days I did not drink, and the last meal of the day was high tea with the ship's officers at 5 p.m., after which I sat in the saloon alone or retired to my cabin where unsecured objects hurled themselves from one side of the floor to the other all night, keeping me from sleep.

Someone else rescued the Spanish ship and eventually we limped into Vigo to sit it out while the storm abated, and sat there for two days, not allowed to go on shore and watched over by two of Franco's policemen in shovel hats. Eventually we reached Leixoes at the mouth of the Douro and the master and I attended matins at St. James's Anglican church, after which he gave me an introduction to the very elegant English Club in Oporto so that I could stay there as an honorary member.

Foreigners (i.e. Portuguese) were not much encouraged in the Club, but port was — as long as it wasn't British port — and drunk at all times of the day, and due to the connoisseurship of the members, was said to be the best port available anywhere in the world, at ridiculously knock-down prices. I gave up not drinking.

Actually the port on board *Convoy* is not at all bad, and they gave me libations of it when I went to a party on it, with a little savoury which Rachel calls Port in a Storm.

On freshly made hot toast spread:
2 oz soft Stilton
½ oz soft unsalted butter
3 turns of the pepper-mill
1 teaspoon Port

mashed together

One of the great fears of the sailor at sea is dying of scurvy through lack of fresh fruit and vegetables and therefore a deficiency of Vitamin C in the body. You simply can't get fresh fruit and vegetables while stuck on the Maplin Sands, though you might have done if they'd built their airport there and Fortes had got the catering concession.

Nowadays *Convoy* always carries a bottle of Rose's Lime Juice, and below are listed a few of the things you can do with it.

Lemon Drink   3 lemons — juice and grated rind
2 lb granulated sugar
1 oz citric acid
2 pts boiling water

Method
Dissolve sugar in water. Add juice, gratings of lemon and citric acid. Leave 2 hours. Strain. Serve with a dash of Rose's Lime Juice and chilled water.

Shortbread   6 oz cornflour
6 oz plain flour
8 oz butter
4 oz castor sugar

Method
Sieve the flours together into a mixing bowl with two pinches of salt. Add sugar and the butter cut into small pieces. Work together as if making pastry. When well mixed squidge lightly into lumps and put on baking tray. Press to ½" level.

Bake at No. 4 gas for about 15 mins till light golden brown. Cool on tin. Slice and sprinkle with sugar.
N.B. It will still be quite soft when cooked. Shortbread hardens when cool.

Serve at 4 p.m. after dropping anchor with a large jug of spiked (vodka, gin) Rose's Lime Juice.

When I first heard that President Reagan was going to dismantle this Salt thing of his, my first reaction was "what a waste after all that money that has been poured into it." It would make an excellent auxiliary supply ship for *Convoy* and stripped of its weaponry could play ducks and drakes with her while they are out at sea.

Indeed to show the Russians we mean no harm, we could make a friendly exchange of Maldon salt for some of theirs from the Siberian salt mines, sailing round the northern shores of Russia and demonstrating that the vessel has been well and truly demilitarised and is now in good, safe hands.

But if the US Navy raise some bureaucratic objection, could we not beach her on the edge of Wandsworth Quay, in the vertical position, as a giant salt cellar to supply both *Convoy*'s needs and the customers at 'The Ship'. Perhaps the propellers could be adapted to grind the salt to varying degrees of fineness as required in cooking.

It would help to compensate for the loss of the Shot Tower on the South Bank and provide a visual counter-balance to the cement-mixing machinery on the other side of the road.

My idea of a 'good' sea voyage is not so much linked to a flat calm as to the standard of food and general amenities on board.

I didn't even mind the peculiar corkscrew motion that afflicted the Spanish Transmeditteraneo Line's steamship's overnight passage from Las Palmas to Arrecife, even though I had to share a large, square cabin with a very seasick Spanish priest and two ditto laymen. The vessel had decent mahogany panelling and served a three-course dinner, and I didn't have to go on with it in the morning to the dreadful Spanish Saharan town of Villa Cisneros.

What I did jib over was the little steamer that linked Belle Ile, off the coast of Brittany, with the French mainland at Quiberon. Once on board, I looked for the refreshment room, with a view to having a pre-lunch drink. There was nothing except a kind of dark cupboard in which the other passengers suffered from *mal de mer,* and the whole outfit, scabrous with blisters of dark-brown rust, stank of bilge-water and decaying fish.

It was an unhappy voyage, but I consoled myself with the thought that when we arrived at the little Vaubanesque port of Le Palais* there would be a choice of restaurants and bars awaiting me.

But first of all I needed a hotel room. The madam in charge looked at me as if I was mad. Did I not know that it was 'out of season'? It was early April, and it transpired that I was the only tourist, foreign or otherwise, on the island. In the end they too provided me with a cupboard. It had matchboarding on the outside and had obviously once been a linen press. The other rooms were being 'done up' in time for the season.

Then I asked about lunch. Lunch was 'off'. It was now 2.45 and 'out of season'. I peered out in the street. All the restaurants were closed, obviously until the season commenced. This was Belle Ile, la Belle France.

*French for 'The Palace': don't know why.

I came back indoors and pleaded. Reluctantly they produced two square slices of cold ham, out of a square tin, with a gherkin and a piece of butterless French bread, plus 37.5 cl of a plangent red wine, all too obviously made somewhere near Villa Cisneros.

Faced by the long afternoon gloom of Le Palais, I tracked down the island's taxi-driver and made him take me to see the ruins of the Divine Sarah's (Sarah Bernhardt) house at the northern tip of the island. En route he pointed out a small grass airfield, to which small planes came when it was not out of season.

There was no return boat that day, but I found a patisserie that served a baba au rhum (with live rum poured out of a scent bottle) and a café crème. No dinner was available, anywhere, and I curled up in the cupboard and went to sleep, catching the rusty boat back in the morning after an elementary breakfast. At least it was warmer than the two nights I had spent previously, trying to sleep in a deck-chair on the deck of a tiny cargo-boat on passage from Funchal to a place called Vila Baleira (there was a taxi here too, a 1926 open American tourer, and its owner-driver was the Mayor of Vila Baleira).

I drove my hired car to Dinan, where I had hired it in the first place, and took to a series of grass airfields and small aeroplanes. First Dinard, then St Brieuc, Jersey (they had given up landing on the beach by this time), Guernsey, Alderney and finally Southampton, still mostly grass. And subsequently back to the Theatre Royal, York, where I could at least go down to the station buffet at any time and eat a sausage roll in one of four selected languages. In French they called it 'paté en croute'.

BOOKS FOR FURTHER READING

Graham, Richard, 'The Good Dog's Cook Book' (Jay Landesman Ltd, 1979, new revised edition Pedigree Books, 1985)

Graham, Richard, 'Cuisine for Cats' (Jay Landesman Ltd, 1980, 3rd and 4th editions Pedigree Books, 1985)

Graham, Richard, 'The Good Dog's Guide to Better Living' (Jay Landesman, 1981)

Heath, Edward, 'Sailing' (Sidgwick & Jackson Ltd, 1975)

McNeill, D. B., TD, PhD, 'Coastal Passenger Steamers and Inland Navigations in the North of Ireland' (Ulster Museum, 1960, 3s 6d. By post 6d extra)